Lever, Screw, and Inclined Plane

Lever, Screw,
and
Inclined Plane

The Power of Simple Machines

By Gare Thompson

NATIONAL GEOGRAPHIC

WASHINGTON D.C.

One of the world's largest nonprofit scientific and educational organizations, the National Geographic Society was founded in 1888 "for the increase and diffusion of geographic knowledge." Fulfilling this mission, the Society educates and inspires millions every day through its magazines, books, television programs, videos, maps and atlases, research grants, the National Geographic Bee, teacher workshops, and innovative classroom materials. The Society is supported through membership dues, charitable gifts, and income from the sale of its educational products. This support is vital to National Geographic's mission to increase global understanding and promote conservation of our planet through exploration, research, and education.

For more information, please call
1-800-NGS-LINE (647-5463) or write to the following address:
National Geographic Society
1145 17th Street N.W.
Washington, D.C. 20036-4688
U.S.A.

For information about special discounts for bulk purchases, please contact
National Geographic Books Special Sales at ngspecsales@ngs.org

Visit the Society's Web site: www.nationalgeographic.com

Copyright © 2006 National Geographic Society

Text revised from *Simple Machines* in the National Geographic Windows on Literacy program from National Geographic School Publishing, © 2002 National Geographic Society

Published by National Geographic Society. Washington, D.C. 20036

Design by Project Design Company

Printed in the United States

Library of Congress Cataloging-in-Publication Data

Thompson, Gare.
  Lever, screw, and inclined plane : the power of simple machines / by Gare Thompson.
    p. cm.
  Includes index.
  ISBN-13: 978-0-7922-5949-7 (library binding)
  ISBN-10: 0-7922-5949-1 (library binding)
  1. Simple machines--Juvenile literature. I. Title.
TJ147.T4835 2006
621.8--dc22

                    2006016328

Photo Credits
Front Cover: © Jeff Smith/ Photographers Choice/ Getty Images; Spine: © Deborah Raven/ Photonica/ Getty Image; Endpaper: © Deborah Raven/ Photonica/ Getty Images; 2-3: © National Geographic/ Getty Images; 6: © Jacob Taposchaner/ Taxi/ Getty Images; 8: © Mel Yates/ Stone/ Getty Images; 10: © Digital Vision/ Getty Images; 12: Photolibrary.com; 14: © Randy Faris/ Corbis; 15 (top): Kenneth Garrett/ National Geographic Image Collection; 16: © Tony Anderson/ PhotoDisc/ Getty Image; 17: Photolibrary.com; 18: © Lindsay Edwards Photography; 19 (top): © Juan Silva/ Iconica/ Getty Images; 20: © Tom Schierlitz/ The Image Bank/ Getty Image; 21: © Lindsay Edwards Photography; 22 (top): © Lindsay Edwards Photography; 22 (bottom): © PhotoDisc/ Getty Images; 23 (top): © AAAC/ Topham/ The Image Works; 24: © Alistair Berg/ Taxi / Getty Images; 25: © Lindsay Edwards Photography; 26: © Photolibrary.com; 27 (top): © Hulton Archive/ Getty Images; 28: © Pete Saloutos/ Corbis; 30: © Philippe Ughetto/ Photo Alto/ Getty Images; 31 (top): © Tom Stewart/ Corbis; 32: Digital Imagery; 33: © Lindsay Edwards Photography; 34: © Jamie Grill/ Iconica/ Getty Images; 35 (top): © Sandra Baker/ The Image Bank/ Getty Images.

Contents

Work

What does work mean to a scientist? Scientists say that work is done when a force is used to move an object over a distance. To do work, you must move something.

Suppose you use force to push on a wall. Are you doing work? No, the wall does not move. What if you push a door and it opens. Now, you are doing work. The door moved. Your push was the force that made the door move. Pushing, pulling, and lifting are the most common forms of work.

Planting a tree is work because you have to push the tree into the soil. The tree has moved into its new home.

Chapter 1

Machines and Work

How can we make work easier? We can use machines. A machine is anything that helps us do work. Machines help us cut things, lift things, and move things.

Some machines are called simple machines. A simple machine is a machine that has few or no moving parts. There are six kinds of simple machines: inclined plane, wedge, screw, lever, wheel and axle, and pulley. Each of these machines reduces the amount of effort needed to do something.

Climbing into a treehouse means work. Using a simple machine makes work easier.

Scissors are a kind of simple machine that makes cutting easier.

A simple machine does one of the following:

- Increases the speed of something
- Reduces the effort needed to do something
- Changes the direction of the force that you use

Let's look at how simple machines help us do work.

The Six Kinds of Simple Machines

Inclined Plane

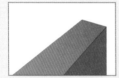

Wedge

Screw

Lever

Wheel and Axle

Pulley

Using a ramp, or inclined plane, makes loading a truck much easier.

Chapter 2

The Inclined Plane

You need to put a large heavy box in the back of a truck. You can't lift it. The box is too heavy. There must be some way to move the box. You see a board. Could you push the box up the board? Yes, that would be easier than lifting it.

You place one end of the board on the ground. You place the other end on the back of the truck. You push the box up into the back of the truck. You use the board as a ramp.

The ramp is a simple machine called an inclined plane. This simple machine doesn't

Rolling the snowball up the hill takes less work than carrying it.

move, but it helps you move things. When you use an inclined plane, you have to move an object a greater distance, but it takes less effort because you need less force.

How We Use Inclined Planes

Look around you and you will see many inclined planes in use. Look for these simple machines when you cross the street. Look for them when you enter buildings in your town. Where else can you see people using inclined planes?

Machines Long Ago and Today

The Inclined Plane

We are not sure how the pyramids in Egypt were built. One idea is that the Egyptians used inclined planes or ramps. The workers pushed the heavy stones up the ramps.

Chapter 3

The Wedge

Did you know you use a
simple machine every time
you dig a hole? A shovel is
a simple machine called
a wedge.

How We Use Wedges

A wedge is used to split or
cut things. A wedge can be

Nearly all cutting
tools use the wedge.

broad and flat like a knife or an ax. A wedge
can also be round and pointed like an arrow.

A shovel is a kind of wedge that we
use to split the ground open.

17

An ax is a heavy wedge. To split wood, you swing the ax downward. The downward force is then changed into a sideways force. The sideways force pushes the wood apart.

When you bite into an apple, your front teeth act as wedges.

Sometimes simple machines are combined to do work. A zipper uses the idea of both the inclined plane and the wedge. The zipper's slide has wedges that open and close the teeth.

Speaking of teeth, did you know that you have wedges in your body? Remember that most wedges are cutting tools. What part of your body do you use to cut things? That's right, your front teeth are wedges!

Machines Long Ago and Today

The Wedge

Farmers used to dig their fields using simple wooden or metal plows pulled by farm animals. As a plow is dragged along, it cuts the ground, pushing the soil aside. Today many farmers use machines powered by engines to do this work.

Using a drill
makes work
easier.

Chapter 4

The Screw

You want to put a shelf in your room. You have a board and a bracket. And you have something else. You have another simple machine called a screw. You can use the screw to attach the bracket to the wall. Then you can hang up your shelf.

Look at the picture of

body

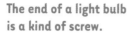
The end of a light bulb
is a kind of screw.

Remember that moving something up an inclined plane takes less force than lifting it straight up. A screw is a twisted inclined plane. So when you turn a screw, you use less force than if you tried to push the screw straight into the wall.

How We Use Screws

Screws do more than just hold things together. A drill is a machine that uses a kind of screw to make holes. The screw moves in and out, creating a hole.

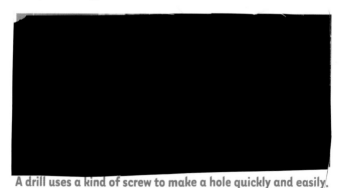

A drill uses a kind of screw to make a hole quickly and easily.

The Screw

Long ago, a Greek scientist named Archimedes invented a lifting screw. It helped farmers water their crops. The lifting screw moved water from a lower level to a higher level. It had a crank attached to a screw. When a farmer turned the crank, water went up the screw and then spilled out.

This simple machine makes play possible.

Chapter 5

The Lever

The lever is another kind of simple machine. A lever is a bar that can be used for lifting. Look at the girl in the picture. She's using the stick as a lever. She puts the stick under a heavy rock. The rock is the load, or the

force

fulcrum   load

object she wants to move. Then she balances the stick on a small rock. The small rock acts as a fulcrum. A fulcrum lets a lever change the direction of a force. So when the girl pushes down on the stick, the heavy rock is pushed up.

How We Use Levers

We use levers to move heavy loads. We also use levers to pry or crack things open. Levers also help us have fun. We use levers when we play baseball or ride on a seesaw.

Every lever can change the direction of a force. But levers can look different. A pair of scissors has two levers that share one fulcrum.

When you swing a bat, your hands are the bat's fulcrum.

The Lever

Some scientists think that the lever was the first machine humans used. Early people used tree branches to move huge rocks. The tree branch was the lever. Another rock was the fulcrum. Pitchforks are a kind of lever that farmers use to move hay.

Chapter 6

The Wheel and Axle

Wheels are all around us. How did you get to school today? Did you ride a bike or take a bus? If you did, then you used a wheel and axle.

The wheel and axle is a simple machine with two parts, a wheel and an axle. The larger wheel turns on a smaller wheel, or post, called an axle. Watch a bike wheel spin. Does it fly off the bike when it spins? No, the wheel stays on the bike because it spins on an axle. The wheel and axle work together to make the bike move with less effort.

On a bike, two wheels and axles work together.

How We Use Wheels and Axles

We all know that cars and other forms of transportation use the wheel and axle, but that's not the only place where this simple machine can be found. Any machine that has parts that move in circles uses wheels and axles. When you open a doorknob or turn on a faucet, you're using a wheel and axle.

Some wheels have grooves, or teeth, on them. These wheels are called gears. The teeth on gears fit together so that one gear turns another.

A lot of gears work together to move the hands on a watch.

The Wheel and Axle

Some scientists say that the wheel is the most important invention of all time. Long ago (and now, too), wheels were used to make pottery. Wheels are also used in almost every machine that helps us travel from place to place.

A pulley is nothing more than a wheel with a rope wrapped around it.

Chapter 7

The Pulley

Have you ever raised a flag? If you have, you have used a simple machine called a pulley. What does a pulley remind you of? Did you guess a wheel? Let's see how a pulley uses a wheel to make work easier.

A pulley is a wheel that has a rope wrapped around it. A pulley changes the direction of a force. With a pulley, you pull down to lift something up. This can make work easier.

Construction workers use pulleys to lift heavy loads.

The flagpole uses a pulley to get the flag to the top.

It's easier to pull down than it is to lift up.

Some pulleys use two wheels instead of one. With these pulleys you still pull down to lift an object up. But using two wheels lets you use less force. The more wheels you use, the less force you have to use to lift an object.

How We Use Pulleys

People often use a pulley to move things that are hard to reach. Remember the flagpole. It's easier to raise a flag using a pulley than it is to climb a tall ladder. Pulleys make life easier.

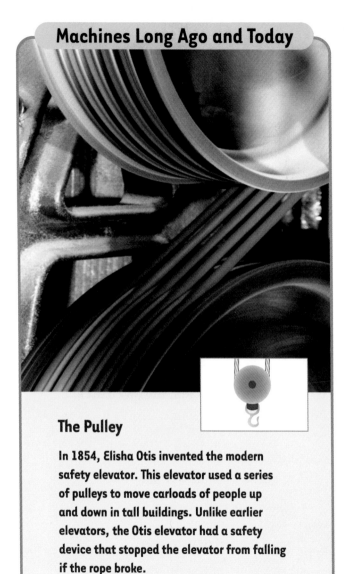

The Pulley

In 1854, Elisha Otis invented the modern safety elevator. This elevator used a series of pulleys to move carloads of people up and down in tall buildings. Unlike earlier elevators, the Otis elevator had a safety device that stopped the elevator from falling if the rope broke.

How to Write an A+ Report

1. Choose a topic.

- Find something that interests you.

- Make sure it is not too big or too small.

2. Find sources.

- Ask your librarian for help.

- Use many different sources: books, magazine articles, and websites.

3. Gather information.

- Take notes. Write down the big ideas and interesting details.

- Use your own words.

4. Organize information.

- Sort your notes into groups that make sense.

- Make an outline. Put your groups of notes in the order you want to write your report.

5. Write your report.

- Write an introduction that tells what the report is about.

- Use your outline and notes as you write to make sure you say everything you want to say in the order you want to say it.

- Write an ending that tells about your report.

- Write a title.

6. Revise and edit your report.

- Read your report to make sure it makes sense.

- Read it again to check spelling, punctuation, and grammar.

7. Hand in your report!

Glossary

axle	a rod that a wheel moves around
force	a push or pull
fulcrum	a fixed point on which a lever turns to change the direction of a force
inclined plane	a simple machine in the shape of a slope that makes moving objects up or down easier
lever	a simple machine made of a bar that turns on a fixed point
load	an object or weight that is moved
machine	something that makes work easier
pulley	a simple machine made of a rope or belt that moves over one or more wheels
screw	a simple machine that is an inclined plane turned in a circle
simple machine	a machine that has few or no moving parts
threads	the ridges on a screw
wedge	a simple machine that makes cutting or splitting an object easier
wheel	a round frame that spins around an axle
work	when a force is used to move an object over a distance

Further Reading

• Books •

Moor, Jo Ellen. *Simple Machines*. Monterey, CA: Evan-Moor Educational Publishers, 1998. Ages 9-12, 80 pages.

Nankivell-Aston, Sally. *Science Experiments With Simple Machines*. London: Franklin Watts, 2000. Ages 9-12, 32 pages.

Tocci, Salvatore. *Experiments With Simple Machines*. Danbury, CT: Children's Press, 2000. Ages 8-10, 48 pages.

Weiss, Harvey. *Machines and How They Work*. New York, NY: Thomas Y. Crowell, 1983. Ages 9-12, 80 pages.

Wells, Robert E. *How Do You Lift a Lion?* Morton Grove, IL: Albert Whitman and Company, 1996. Ages 9-12, 32 pages.

• Websites •

EdHeads
http://edheads.org/activities/simple-machines/

Enchanted Learning
http://www.enchantedlearning.com/physics/machines/Levers.shtml

The Franklin Institute Online
http://sln.fi.edu/qa97/spotlight3/spotlight3.html

The Museum of Science
http://www.mos.org/sln/Leonardo/InventorsToolbox.html

Pieces of Science
http://www.fi.edu/pieces/knox/automaton/simple.htm

Scholastic Online Activities
http://teacher.scholastic.com/dirtrep/simple/

ThinkQuest
http://library.thinkquest.org/J002079F/sub3.htm

University of Utah
http://sunshine.chpc.utah.edu/javalabs/java12/machine/stdntovrvw.htm

Wikipedia Online Encyclopedia
http://en.wikipedia.org/wiki/Simple_machines

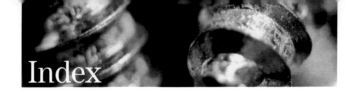

Index